HORSES
& PONIES

First published in Great Britain by
CAXTON EDITIONS
an imprint of
The Caxton Book Company,
16 Connaught Street,
Marble Arch, London, W2 2AF.

ISBN 1 84067 060 6

A copy of the CIP data for this book is available from the British Library upon request.

With grateful thanks to Morse Modaberi who designed this book.

Created and produced for Caxton Editions by
FLAME TREE PUBLISHING,
a part of The Foundry Creative Media Company Ltd,
Crabtree Hall, Crabtree Lane,
Fulham, London, SW6 6TY.

Printed in Singapore by Star Standard Industries Pte. Ltd.

HORSES & PONIES

*Favourite Breeds of
these Beautiful Animals,
Explained in Glorious Colour*

MAUREEN HILL

CAXTON EDITIONS

⇀ Contents ↽

Introduction

Humans have used horses for thousands of years; there are cave paintings more than 15,000 years old which show pictures of horses. At first horses and ponies were domesticated for their milk and meat. Later, people realised they were good animals for pulling and carrying heavy loads. Some time later men began to ride them; we have pictures of men on horseback as far back as 2000 BC.

Horses and ponies have played a very important part in human development. For hundreds of years they were a main source of power for heavy agricultural and building work, and a means of transport for both people and goods. They were also important in warfare: carrying heavily armoured knights in the Middle Ages and carrying cavalry soldiers and pulling cannon and carts in later wars. Throughout the world, most of these jobs have now been taken over by machines, but there are still many countries where the horse has an important role in agriculture, by pulling ploughs and carts.

Horses and ponies are the same species of animal. The main difference between them is size. Horses and ponies are measured in 'hands'; a 'hand' is a measure of four inches (10 cm) and they are measured from the hoof to the withers, or shoulder. Ponies usually measure under 14.2 hands and are also more compact in build than horses, with a rougher coat and smaller ears.

Evolution of the Horse

Horses and ponies evolved from a small creature the size of a fox. This creature, named Hyracotherium, lived about 50 million years ago and fed on leaves. Over the years the horse's teeth adapted to enable it to feed on grass – modern horses are still vegetarian.

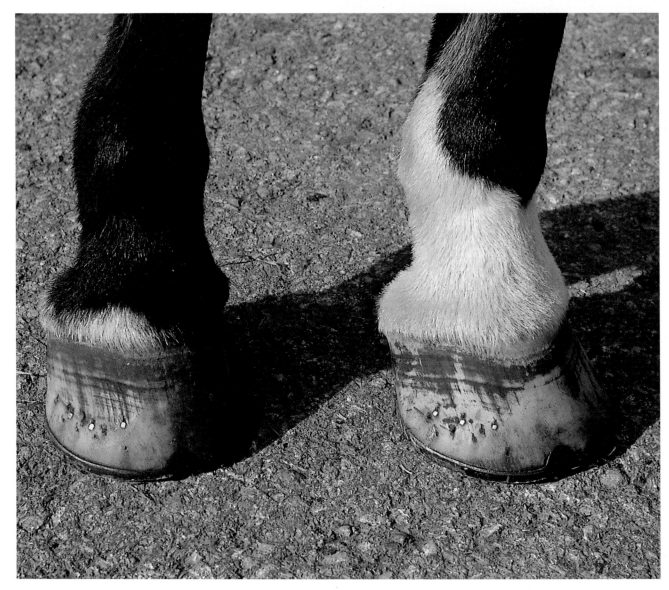

Hyracotherium had four toes on its front feet and three on its back feet. The need to be able to run fast to escape from predators meant the horse had to be able to move on tiptoe. Over millions of years, the outside toes disappeared, as they were not needed, leaving the modern horse with just a single hoof on each foot.

Different types of horses and ponies developed depending upon the environment and climate they were in. There are two wide classifications, the hot-blooded group from the southern countries and the cold-blooded group from the northern countries. Hot- and cold-blooded refers to the horse's temperament and build. For example, the cold-blooded group are horses and ponies descended from prehistoric Central European horses which were stocky and heavy-set. Interbreeding of the two groups has produced a third group, the warm-blooded group.

Horses and ponies have been domesticated for thousands of years, which means that humans have had an effect on their original breeding patterns. In the last 300 years in particular, humans have tried to improve and develop many different breeds for different tasks and situations.

Human influence on horses and ponies has been so great that there are no longer any truly wild horses left in their natural environment. Przewalski's Horse was the last known type of wild horse, but now it only exists in zoos.

The Modern Horse

The 'points' of a horse or pony are the various parts of its external body, ranging from its muzzle – the mouth and nose area – to the dock – the bony part of the tail from which the tail hair grows. Experts consider all these points when looking at the 'conformation' of a horse or pony. By looking at the relationship of all the points to one another, it is possible to judge how well suited an animal will be to the task required of them.

Horses are quite long-lived animals, living for between 20 to 40 years. It is possible to tell the age of a horse by looking at the six incisor teeth at the front of the mouth. Up until the age of eight these teeth go through yearly changes. After the age of eight, it is more difficult to be accurate as to exact age.

It is possible for horses and ponies to have foals from the age of two but most breeders prefer to wait until the animals are at least three years old. The 'stallion', the male horse,

will father offspring with several female horses, or 'mares'. A mare's pregnancy lasts about 11 months after which she will give birth to a single foal, called a 'filly' if it is female and a 'colt' if it is male. It is extremely rare for a mare to have twins.

It is important to remember that the modern horse is a domesticated animal and, as such, needs to be cared for by humans throughout its life. It needs to be given shelter, access to food and attention if it is injured or ill.

Colouring and Markings

The most common colours of horse are: Bay, a yellowish or reddish brown; Chestnut (sometimes called Sorrel), which is a ginger or yellowish red colour; Grey, which can vary from almost white to quite a dark grey; Brown, which is a much darker brown than a bay; and Black. Some horses are mixtures or variations of these colours. If it is unclear what colour the horse's coat is then the colour on the tips of the ears, the muzzle, mane tail and the lower leg will help decide. In some horses these areas are different to the main body colour. For example a bay horse may be black on these areas.

A Strawberry Roan is a chestnut horse with a sprinkling of white. Skewbald horses have large patches of white mixed with patches of any other colour except black. Black and white patches produce a Piebald horse. Some horses, like the American Appaloosa, are grey spotted with different colours. One of the most beautiful horses is the Palomino; a golden coloured coat with a straw-coloured mane and tail.

On single-coloured horses white markings can sometimes be found on the body, head and legs. Patches of white in the saddle or girth areas are the commonest body marking. The most common face markings are: a narrow Stripe down the centre of the face; a wider marking than the stripe called a Blaze; a Star, which is a white mark on the forehead; and a Snip, a small, white streak on the nose.

White socks and stockings are the most frequently seen leg markings but streaks of white can be confined to small areas like the heel or pastern.

Horses in Motion

There are four basic 'gaits', or paces, at which a horse or pony can move and they can be identified by the rhythm of the beat of the hooves.

The 'walk' is the slowest gait and has a four-beat rhythm. The left foreleg moves forward, followed by the right hind leg, the right foreleg then moves forward, followed by the left hind leg.

A 'trot' produces a much faster pace and has a two-beat rhythm because two legs move and strike the ground at the same time. The left foreleg and right hind leg leave the ground together and, while they are in the air, the other two legs leave the ground. A rider using an English saddle has to compensate for this by rising out of the saddle until the hooves are touching the ground; this is called 'posting'.

The 'canter' is faster still and more complicated. It has a three-beat rhythm and has either a left or right foreleg lead. The sequence of movement for a left lead is that the right leg moves first, this is followed by the left hind leg and right foreleg moving together and finally the 'leading' left foreleg leaves the ground.

Galloping' is a faster version of the canter but has four beats as each hoof strikes the ground individually.

Horses and ponies can be trained to have slight variations on these gaits, including a high-stepping gait. The Tennessee Walker horse has been bred to have a very smooth and distinctive gait to avoid jarring the rider in the saddle.

Horses and Ponies in the Past

For hundreds of years the horse and pony provided the main means of transportation of both goods and people. People might ride their own horse or pony or travel in a horse-drawn carriage, stagecoach or simply on the back of a cart.

Carts were principally used for moving goods, often to market. The need to transport larger and heavier goods came about with the Industrial Revolution in Britain, and saw the development of the canal system. Canal barges were pulled along the towpath by extremely strong Heavy horses.

A visit to London in Victorian times would have demonstrated the importance of the horse to the society. There would have been individual riders, people in their own carriages, horse-drawn cabs for hire, horse-drawn trams and delivery wagons going to and from shops, pubs and wealthy homes. There were an estimated 30,000 horses in the capital at the time, which created a huge problem of how to clear the tonnes of horse manure from the streets!

Outside the city centre, horses and ponies were vital to farms and factories. Small ponies even worked underground in the mines; most of them were stabled underground and did not see any daylight until they retired.

In the USA, the horse was an important tool in colonising the continent. The wagons that made the trek west were pulled by horses which were then used for farming the newly settled land. The Pony Express became a legend – it carried the mail 2,000 miles across the USA in just 10 days, a feat unimagined until that time. Each pony was ridden at full gallop for 15 miles before the mail and rider were transferred to another, fresh pony for the next 15 miles.

Arabs and Thoroughbreds

The Arab, or Arabian horse, is the oldest and purest breed known. Written records of their breeding have been kept for more than a thousand years, and it is known that the desert tribesmen who bred them for thousands of years previously kept the breed pure by passing on records by word of mouth. The Arabian horse was used during Muslim invasions which helped spread the Islamic faith in the 7th and 8th centuries, and as a result it was crossbred with local breeds in North Africa and Southern Europe.

However these new breeds were never taken home to mix with the pure Arab strain.

The hot-blooded Arab is said to be the most beautiful and elegant horse in the world and has been used to improve the pedigree of several breeds. It is long-lived and has great stamina, speed and intelligence.

One of the most important roles the Arab horse has fulfilled is to help in the development of the Thoroughbred horse used throughout the world in horse racing. At the beginning of the 18th century, three Arab stallions were imported into Britain – the Byerley Turk, the Darley and Godolphin Arabians. From these three horses the Thoroughbred was developed by crossing them with other horses bred for racing.

Arab horses are now bred throughout the world although the difference in environments they are raised in can create a slightly different horse. The American Arab is much larger than a horse bred in the desert. The King of Jordan has set up a Stud Farm where the smaller, pure breed can be raised.

Heavy Horses

Heavy horses were developed to undertake heavy work of all kinds. In Europe and Asia there are many breeds, for example: the Italian Avelignese, the German Schleswig, the Danish Jutland, the Russian Vladimir and the French Percheron, although France has more breeds of Heavy horse than any other country.

British Heavy horses were developed from crossing Heavy horses imported from Europe with native horses for war. The British Shire horse was first used to carry knights in armour; the weight of the armour and weapons was too much for an ordinary horse. A Shire horse can stand higher than 18 hands and is the largest Heavy horse in the world, able to pull as much as five tonnes.

On farms, Shire horses were important for pulling ploughs and farm carts. The Suffolk Punch, now much reduced in numbers, was an important farm horse on East Anglia. Although at 16 hands it is smaller than a Shire it can weigh over one tonne, the same as a Shire. Suffolk Punches are always chestnut in colour and do not have the 'feathers', long hairs around the fetlock, that many other Heavy horses have.

During the 18th century in the Clyde Valley in Scotland, breeders developed the Clydesdale horse for use in farming and as a draught horse. Draught horses are those that pull loads; they can be put to work pulling such things as canal barges, drays, wagons and trams. Clydesdales stand at 16–17 hands and have great strength and stamina but, like many Heavy horses, have a pleasant temperament which makes them easy to handle despite their size.

Riding Horses

Thoroughbred horses are bred to be ridden but they are difficult to handle and are best suited to racing. However, a Thoroughbred crossed with an Arab, to give what is called an Anglo-Arab, is an excellent horse for many sports – eventing, show-jumping, hacking.

The German Hanoverian horse owes its development to George I.

Although king of Britain, he was originally from Hanover in Germany. He sent many British Thoroughbreds there to breed with local horses in an attempt to produce an all-round horse, suitable for riding, pulling light carriages and draught work.

In the USA, the classic cowboy horse is the Quarter horse which was developed by breeding English Thoroughbreds with the Spanish horses that colonised America. The horse gets its name from the time when it was regularly raced along the main street of many American towns – these streets were usually quarter of a mile long. Quarter horses are still used for racing, but are also often seen in rodeos.

Another American horse breed is the Morgan, which developed from just one horse owned by Justin Morgan in the late 18th century. This horse showed all round exceptional abilities. When mated with a number of different mares he passed on to a new generation all of those abilities and established a new breed.

One of the oldest breeds of horse in Europe is the Andalusian from Spain. Bred from crosses between Barbs from North Africa and native horses, the Andalusian was once the most prized horse in Europe. Most commonly grey in colour, it is an excellent riding horse that is strong, swift, sure-footed and pleasant in temperament.

Ponies

Although there are a number of ponies of no specific breed, there are also a large number of distinct pony breeds throughout the world, in Europe in particular.

The Haflinger pony, which is a chestnut with a straw-coloured mane and tail, comes from the Tyrol, a mountainous area in Austria, and it is a strong and sure-footed animal.

In Norway, the dun-coloured (yellowish) native Fjord pony looks very like the ponies of the Ice Age with its short-cropped mane.

Criollo ponies are found in South America and are tough ponies used to surviving in poor conditions. They can grow as large as 15 hands and are very popular as polo ponies.

The British Isles has nine native pony breeds, a large number for such a small area. The largest, at up to 14.2 hands, is the Highland Pony, which comes from the highlands and islands of Scotland. It is a popular trekking pony but has also been used as a pack pony and a draught animal in the past.

Welsh ponies are divided into four types, called Sections A, B, C and D. All types make excellent riding ponies and the larger types can also be used for driving – that is pulling a light vehicle.

The Dale pony is also a good driving pony, as it is strong and stocky, but is also used for riding and trekking. Dale ponies are rather like a small version of the Heavy horse, complete with feathers. The Fell pony is very similar; although slightly smaller and with a lighter build. It has the same colouring as the Dale pony – dark brown or black.

Miniature Horses and Ponies

The Shetland pony is the smallest breed of pony in the world and is usually about 9.2 hands high; it should not be bigger than 10.2 hands. They are often black or brown and are long-lived, extremely strong and hardy animals, able to survive winters in the often-frozen Shetland Islands, where they may have to survive on a diet of nothing but seaweed. Their thick, rough winter coat turns to a smooth one in summer and they have long manes and tails.

They are very popular as children's ponies, although many people doubt their suitability for this as they have a wide girth which can be difficult for young children to straddle comfortably. They can be quite wilful and difficult to control, especially for an inexperienced rider.

Although smaller than a pony, the Falabella is actually a miniature horse. It should not be more than 7.2 hands high and can be any colour, including piebald and skewbald. The Falabella was bred in Argentina by crossing Thoroughbreds with Shetland ponies. They are popular in the USA as a child's first pony, but are not very strong.

Another miniature horse is the Caspian, an ancient breed which was very recently close to extinction in Iran. A breeding programme has since been established to increase numbers of this elegant animal. Although it is only about 10 hands high, the Caspian looks like a Thoroughbred. Genetic testing has suggested it may be an ancestor of the Arab horse, making it one of the oldest known breeds. It is a good-tempered horse with strength and speed.

Wild Horses

There are no longer any truly wild populations of horse or pony left in the world, but there are several groups of wild animals that have either returned to the wild or are partially wild.

In America there are herds of 'wild' Mustangs. These horses became wild after having been bred as domestic horses. They were introduced by the Spanish in the 16th century, and were lost, abandoned or escaped into the wilderness. They have since bred into tough, smaller versions of the original breeds which were of Spanish and Arab descent. The Native Americans at first hunted them for meat but soon realised they were most useful for riding to hunt buffalo. The Nez Percé Indians developed their own breed called the Appaloosa from these Mustangs.

Although often referred to as horses, the beautiful animals of the Camargue in France are in fact ponies. They can be as big as 15 hands and adults are white in colour, although the foals are born brown. Camargue ponies are descended from a prehistoric breed crossed with Arabs and Barbs. They live on salt marshes where the grazing is sparse and tough,

developing a hardy and strong animal. A few of the ponies are broken in by local 'cowboys' who use them to herd the black Camargue bulls.

In Britain, some of the native pony breeds are semi-wild. The ponies of the New Forest, Dartmoor and Exmoor are left to roam free, but every year some are rounded up to be broken in and a check is kept on the others.

Horses at Work Today

Fewer horses work today in Britain than in previous centuries and it is also rare to see horses used for transportation. However, a few farms still use horses for ploughing and some cities and towns have horse-drawn carriages to take tourists around the sights.

A police horse is the most likely working horse people will come into contact with. Many countries have mounted police; the most famous is probably the Royal Canadian Mounted Police, nicknamed the 'Mounties'.

British police horses are used mainly for crowd control at events such as football matches and demonstrations. The horses are trained to be calm despite noisy crowds, waving flags and banners, fireworks, sirens or brass bands. They also have to learn to stand still in a pushing crowd and to walk over people lying down without treading on them.

Police horses are often present at ceremonial events. During the annual Lord Mayor's Parade, six grey Shire horses pull the new Lord Mayor of London's four-and-a-half-tonne coach through the streets of the City. At the Trooping of the Colour, at Horse Guards Parade in London, it is

possible to see many of the cavalry horses of the British Army. These horses are no longer used in battle, but appear for ceremonial duties and in displays, such as the Royal Tournament.

The circus is another area in which one can see working horses. There are three basic types of circus horse – the high-school horse that performs dressage type movements and other more spectacular movements; the liberty horse, seen dressed in plumes and fancy harnesses and working in synchronised groups and the rosin back or 'vaulting horse', on which a bareback rider performs tricks.

Ponies at Work Today

Like horses, some ponies are still in use on farms or used to pull light tourist vehicles, but the majority of working ponies are to be found in the numerous riding schools up and down the country. Most riding schools will have a range of ponies, from the small and quiet-tempered pony for the young novice rider to the larger, livelier pony for the older, more experienced rider. However, all riding school ponies should be even-tempered and should be used to being ridden and handled by a variety of riders and carers.

Pony trekking is an increasingly popular pastime. A rider can choose to take a pony trek lasting just a few days or go on a holiday based at a pony trekking centre at which treks are taken each day and where novice

riders can learn about riding and the care of ponies. There are several pony trekking centres in Britain, usually based in beautiful countryside in areas such as Scotland, Wales, the Lake District and Dartmoor. It is also possible to find pony trekking holidays abroad, in countries such as Iceland and France.

The Highland pony is a popular pony for trekking, especially in Scotland where it is still used for carrying deer down from the mountains on hunting expeditions. Another popular breed is the Dales pony. Both these breeds are larger than other British ponies and so are suitable for carrying both adult and child riders.

Ponies also take part in circus acts, often as part of a clown act, demonstrating their intelligence against the foolishness of the clowns.

Horses and Ponies in Sport

Horse racing is said to be the 'sport of kings' and usually only wealthy people can afford to be owners. Racehorses are extremely expensive animals but the horse racing industry in Britain also generates millions of pounds and provides thousands of jobs in training and caring for the horses, managing and running racecourses and staffing betting shops both on and off the course. It is a sport with a huge following and most race meetings attract large crowds, none larger than that seen at the Epsom Derby. There are two types of horse race: Flat Races, where the horses run a level course, and Steeplechases, where the horses have to leap over jumps as well as run.

Speed is the essential quality of flat racing and, to a large extent, steeplechasing, but there are other sports which test the other abilities of horses. Dressage is an event which tests the rider's ability and control of the horse. It requires intense training and intelligence on the part of both the rider and the horse.

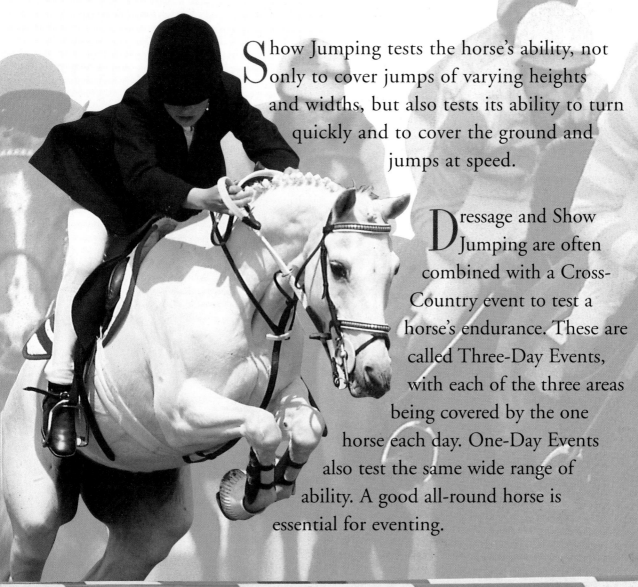

Show Jumping tests the horse's ability, not only to cover jumps of varying heights and widths, but also tests its ability to turn quickly and to cover the ground and jumps at speed.

Dressage and Show Jumping are often combined with a Cross-Country event to test a horse's endurance. These are called Three-Day Events, with each of the three areas being covered by the one horse each day. One-Day Events also test the same wide range of ability. A good all-round horse is essential for eventing.

Polo is a sport in which the horse's job is to carry the rider over the polo ground as the rider seeks to score a goal by hitting the ball through the goal posts at either end of the 275-metre long pitch. In this ancient sport (it is known to have been played as far back as 600 BC) there are four players on each side. The players hit the ball with a polo stick, shaped like a long-handled mallet.

The animals used for polo are actually called ponies, but many of them have been bred to be much larger than pony height, usually about 15 hands. The ponies (and riders) wear protective gear and often have their manes hogged (cut short) and their tails plaited to avoid them interfering with play.

Racing a Four-in-Hand was a popular pastime in the early 19th century; today, although horses are no longer needed to pull vehicles every day, carriage driving has

been revived once again as a sport. Among the best horses for carriage driving are the Hackney and the Cleveland Bay which were bred specifically for harness work. The Hackney has a notable high-stepping but graceful gait.

For children and young people, a Gymkhana is probably the most likely way in which they and their pony will take part in competition. The ponies have to be trained well to take part in the many games, jumping competitions and races at the Gymkhana. These also help to develop the rider's skills in controlling the pony sensitively.

Famous Horses

In Ancient Greece, Alexander the Great's favourite horse was named Bucephalus. Alexander, a renowned horseman, was given this, supposedly unrideable, horse when he was 13 years old. He managed to tame him and together they went on to conquer much of the world.

In Ancient Rome, the Emperor Caligula also had a favourite horse who he made a Consul (or nobleman).

This century, several racehorses have captured the public imagination. The most famous flat race horse was Nijinsky who won the 'Triple Crown', the 2,000 Guineas, the Derby and the St Leger.

Arkle was one of the most famous steeplechase horses – only once failing to gain a 'place' (being one of the first four horses) in a race. After his death, a bronze statue of him was erected at Cheltenham Racecourse.

The greatest horse character of recent years is probably Red Rum, who won the Grand National a record three times. However, he is best known for his lively character, his courage (shown in coming back as a winner, following a foot problem that usually puts horses out of racing) and for his relationship with jockey Bob Champion who also fought back against illness, beating cancer to win the Grand National (on a horse called Aldaniti).

While many individual horses have become famous, one particular breed has become renowned for its skill: the Lipizzaner horses of the Spanish Riding School in Vienna. The breed was established in 1580, when Spanish horses were first imported into Austria, and the School uses stallions bred at its own stud, who grow up in Austria's most beautiful countryside. The foals are born dark brown, but mature to become white. They are an intelligent, strong breed that can have a working life of more than 20 years.

Further Information

Places to Visit

Badminton Horse Trials, Badminton House, near Tetbury, Gloucestershire. Telephone (Tetbury Tourist Information): 01454 218732 – held each year in May.

Burghley Horse Trials, Burghley House, Stamford, Lincolnshire PE9 3JY. Telephone: 01780 752131 – held each year in early September, Thursday through to Sunday.

Royal Tournament, Earls Court, Warwick Road, London SW5. Telephone: 0171 373 8141 – held each year in July.

Shire Horse Centre, Cherry Garden Lane, Maidenhead Thicket, Maidenhead, Berkshire SL6 3QD. Telephone 01628 824848.

Trooping the Colour, Horse Guards Parade, London. Telephone (London Tourist Information): 0171 370 7744 – held each year in early June.

Important Names & Addresses

Riding for the Disabled Association, National Agricultural Centre, Stoneleigh, Kenilworth, Warwickshire CV8 2LR. Telephone: 01203 696510.

British Horse Society, Stoneleigh, Kenilworth, Warwickshire CV8 2LR. Telephone: 01926 707700 – membership available.

National Pony Society, Willingdon House, 102 High Street, Alton, Hampshire GU34 1EN. Telephone: 01420 88333 – membership available.

International League for the Protection of Horses, Colvin House, Snetterton, Norwich, Norfolk NR16 2LR. Telephone: 01953 498682.

Further Reading

Horses & Ponies: Photoguide by Deborah Gill, Collins Gem
The Encyclopedia of the Horse by Elwyn Hartley Edwards, Dorling Kindersley
The Horse by Jane Kidd, Tiger Books International
The Complete Book of Horse & Pony Care by Mike Janson & Juliana Kemball Williams, Parragon Books
Black Beauty by Anna Sewell
Follyfoot and other books in the same series by Monica Dickens
Ponies at the Point by Lucy Daniels
Jill's Gymkhana and other books in the same series by Ruby Ferguson

Picture Credits

All pictures courtesy of **Bob Langrish** except:
Allsport pp. 42, 43
Ann Ronan Picture Library pp. 20-21